OUR SOLAR SYSTEM
SATURN
THE RINGED PLANET

by Mari Schuh

pogo

Ideas for Parents and Teachers

Pogo Books let children practice reading informational text while introducing them to nonfiction features such as headings, labels, sidebars, maps, and diagrams, as well as a table of contents, glossary, and index.

Carefully leveled text with a strong photo match offers early fluent readers the support they need to succeed.

Before Reading

• "Walk" through the book and point out the various nonfiction features. Ask the student what purpose each feature serves.

• Look at the glossary together. Read and discuss the words.

Read the Book

• Have the child read the book independently.

• Invite him or her to list questions that arise from reading.

After Reading

• Discuss the child's questions. Talk about how he or she might find answers to those questions.

• Prompt the child to think more. Ask: Saturn is known as the ringed planet. Its rings are made of ice and rock. Why is Saturn so cold?

Pogo Books are published by Jump!
5357 Penn Avenue South
Minneapolis, MN 55419
www.jumplibrary.com

Library of Congress Cataloging-in-Publication Data

Names: Schuh, Mari C., 1975- author.
Title: Saturn : the ringed planet / by Mari Schuh.
Description: Minneapolis, MN: Jump!, Inc., [2023]
Series: Our solar system | Includes index.
Audience: Ages 7-10
Identifiers: LCCN 2022024568 (print)
LCCN 2022024569 (ebook)
ISBN 9798885243674 (hardcover)
ISBN 9798885243681 (paperback)
ISBN 9798885243698 (ebook)
Subjects: LCSH: Saturn (Planet)—Juvenile literature.
Classification: LCC QB671 .S38 2023 (print)
LCC QB671 (ebook)
DDC 523.46—dc23/eng20220826
LC record available at https://lccn.loc.gov/2022024568
LC ebook record available at https://lccn.loc.gov/2022024569

Editor: Jenna Gleisner
Designer: Emma Bersie

Photo Credits: 3quarks/iStock, cover; Claudio Caridi/Shutterstock, 1; 24K-Production/Shutterstock, 3; Nowwy Jirawat/Shutterstock, 4; World History Archive/Alamy, 5; Shutterstock, 6-7; viktorov.pro/Shutterstock, 8-9; Artsiom P/Shutterstock, 10; NASA/JPL/Space Science Institute, 11, 18-19bl, 19-19br; Dotted Yeti/Shutterstock, 12-13 (Saturn); Maliflower73/Shutterstock, 12-13 (background); NASA Goddard, 14-15; NASA, 16; Federico Emilio/Shutterstock, 17; NASA/JPL-Caltech/SSI, 18-19 (top); Vadim Sadovski/Shutterstock, 20-21, 23.

Printed in the United States of America at Corporate Graphics in North Mankato, Minnesota.

TABLE OF CONTENTS

CHAPTER 1
Saturn in the Sky.............................4

CHAPTER 2
All About Saturn...........................10

CHAPTER 3
Amazing Discoveries.....................16

ACTIVITIES & TOOLS
Try This!.......................................22
Glossary.......................................23
Index...24
To Learn More...............................24

CHAPTER 1

SATURN IN THE SKY

Have you ever looked up at the night sky? Maybe you saw stars. You might have seen the **planet** Saturn, too! You can see it without a **telescope**.

Saturn

Galileo Galilei was an **astronomer**. He made history in 1610. He was the first person to see Saturn with a telescope.

Galileo Galilei

telescope

Saturn is the second largest planet in our **solar system**. How big is it? About 750 Earths could fit inside Saturn.

Earth

TAKE A LOOK!

Saturn is the sixth planet from the Sun. Take a look!

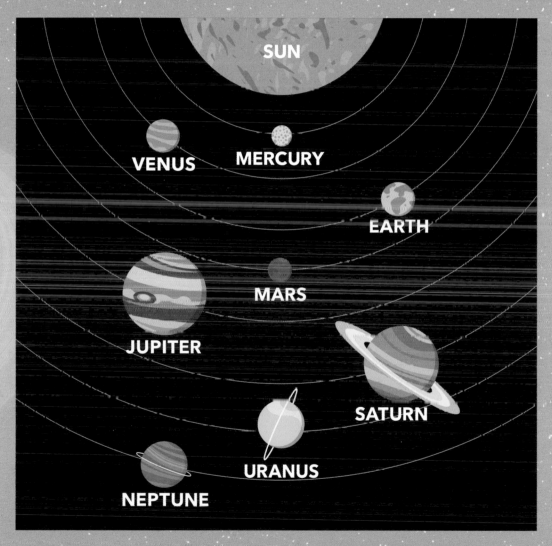

SUN

VENUS

MERCURY

EARTH

MARS

JUPITER

SATURN

URANUS

NEPTUNE

Saturn is known for the rings that circle it. They are made of pieces of ice and rock. Some pieces are as tiny as specks of sand. Others are as big as homes.

rings

CHAPTER 2

ALL ABOUT SATURN

Saturn is very cold. Why? It is far from the Sun. It does not get much sunlight. Its average temperature is –288 degrees Fahrenheit (–178 degrees Celsius). *Brrr!*

Saturn has a thick **atmosphere**. It has three layers of clouds. The outermost layer is the coldest. Its clouds look like colored stripes. Strong winds blow on Saturn. They are stronger than **hurricane** winds on Earth.

Saturn is very different from Earth. We can't stand on Saturn. Why not? Saturn is made up mostly of gases. Its main gases are helium and hydrogen. Hot liquid metal is under the layers of gas. Saturn's **core** is likely hot and rocky.

What is Saturn made of? Take a look at its layers!

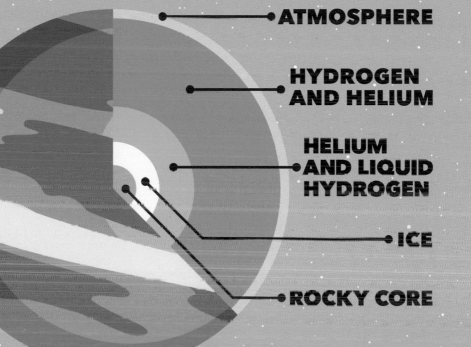

- ATMOSPHERE
- HYDROGEN AND HELIUM
- HELIUM AND LIQUID HYDROGEN
- ICE
- ROCKY CORE

Titan

Titan is Saturn's largest moon. It is the only moon in the solar system known to have clouds. It rains on Titan. This moon also has rivers and lakes.

CHAPTER 3

AMAZING DISCOVERIES

In 1979, *Pioneer 11* made history. It became the first **spacecraft** to fly by Saturn. It studied the planet up close. It sent data and images to Earth. Scientists studied them.

Pioneer 11

In 1981, *Voyager 2* also flew by Saturn. It discovered small rings within the main rings. It took images of them.

Voyager 2

In 2009, the *Cassini* spacecraft discovered something about Saturn's rings. They have vertical shapes in them. The shapes seem to be **particles** that piled up. They created bumps.

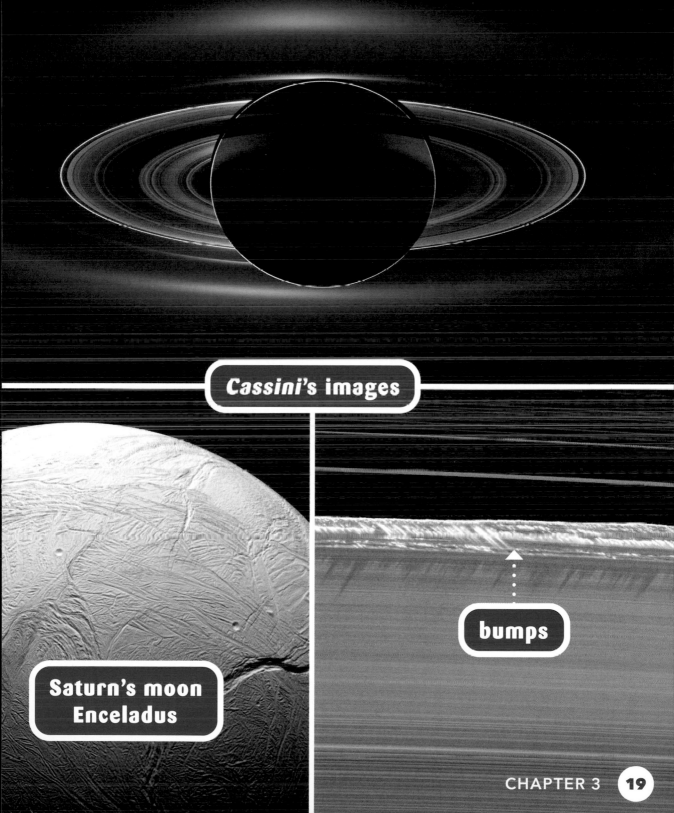

Cassini's images

Saturn's moon Enceladus

bumps

In 2019, scientists discovered 20 more moons near Saturn. How? Better computers helped them review images of the planet. We now know Saturn has at least 82 moons.

Saturn is an amazing planet. What more would you like to discover about it?

DID YOU KNOW?

No planet is known to have more moons than Saturn!

ACTIVITIES & TOOLS

TRY THIS!

DOES SATURN FLOAT?

Saturn is mostly made of gas. It is light for its size. See what it would do in water with this fun activity!

What You Need:

- two balloons of different colors, such as red and blue
- sand
- large container
- water

① Blow up the red balloon with air. Tie it shut. This balloon is Saturn.

② Fill the blue balloon with sand. Tie it shut. This balloon is Earth.

③ Fill a large container with water.

④ Put both balloons in the water. What happens? Does Earth sink or float? Does Saturn sink or float? Why do you think this is?

GLOSSARY

astronomer: A scientist who studies stars, planets, and space.

atmosphere: The mixture of gases that surrounds a planet.

core: The center, most inner part of a planet.

density: The measure of how heavy or light an object is for its size. Density is measured by dividing an object's mass by its volume.

gravity: The force that pulls things toward the center of a planet and keeps them from floating away.

hurricane: A very powerful storm with extremely high winds and heavy rain.

mass: The amount of physical matter an object has.

particles: Extremely small pieces or amounts of matter.

planet: A large body that orbits, or travels in circles around, the Sun.

solar system: The Sun, together with its orbiting bodies, such as the planets, their moons, and asteroids, comets, and meteors.

spacecraft: Vehicles that travel in space.

telescope: A device that uses lenses or mirrors in a long tube to make faraway objects appear bigger and closer.

INDEX

atmosphere 11, 13

Cassini 18

clouds 11, 15

cold 10, 11

core 12, 13

Earth 6, 7, 8, 11, 12, 16

Galilei, Galileo 5

gases 12, 13

gravity 8

ice 8, 13

layers 11, 12, 13

moons 15, 21

Pioneer 11 16

rings 8, 17, 18

rock 8, 12, 13

solar system 6, 7, 15

Sun 7, 10

telescope 4, 5

temperature 10

Titan 15

Voyager 2 17

winds 11

TO LEARN MORE

Finding more information is as easy as 1, 2, 3.

1 Go to www.factsurfer.com

2 Enter "Saturn" into the search box.

3 Choose your book to see a list of websites.

FACT SURFER